The Story of the Sermon on the Mount

Illustrated by Sherry Neidigh

Retold by
Tama M. Montgomery

A Word to Parents and Friends

This story is one of a series of biblical stories especially written, illustrated, and designed to explain a difficult concept in a gentle and simple manner.

Even the youngest child will understand the timeless lessons inherent in each Bible story. Most of all, preschoolers, beginning readers, and older children will enjoy hearing and reading these exciting accounts of heroes from one of the oldest and most exciting books of all: the Holy Bible.

 Ideals Children's Books • Nashville, Tennessee
an imprint of Hambleton-Hill Publishing, Inc.

ISBN 1-57102-109-4

Jesus, the Son of God, traveled throughout the land of Galilee. He healed the sick and worked many wonderful miracles. Most importantly, he brought a new message to the people, a message about God.

Jesus taught his message in the Jewish temples, in the homes of his followers, and even in the streets. The news about him spread quickly, and great crowds of people came to hear him speak.

When Jesus saw all the people, he climbed up on the side of a mountain and sat down. His disciples came and sat with him, as the crowds gathered around. Then Jesus began to teach them, saying:

"Blessed are the poor in spirit, for theirs is the kingdom of heaven.

"Blessed are those who weep, for they shall laugh.

"Blessed are the meek, for they shall inherit the earth.

"Blessed are those who hunger and thirst for righteousness, for they shall be filled.

"Blessed are the merciful, for they shall be shown mercy.

"Blessed are the pure in heart, for they shall see God.

"Blessed are the peacemakers, for they shall be called the children of God.

"Blessed are those who are persecuted for the sake of righteousness, for theirs is the kingdom of heaven.

"Remember, you are the light of the world. No one lights a candle and puts it under a basket so that its light cannot be seen. Instead, you put it on a stand, so that the light shines for everyone in the house.

"Let your light shine like a candle for all the world, so that people will see your good works and give glory to your Father in heaven.

"Don't do a good deed for someone just so that others will say how good you are. If you do, then you already have your reward. God will not reward you again in heaven.

"And when you give to the poor, give in secret. God will see you, and he will reward you openly.

"Do not store up treasures on earth. Rust and moths will destroy these treasures, and thieves will steal them. Instead, store up treasures in heaven. For wherever your treasure is, that is where your heart will be also.

"Do not worry about your life or what you will eat and drink. See the birds of the air. They do not plant seeds or harvest crops or store food in barns, but God feeds them. Aren't you much more important than these birds?

"And why do you worry about what you will wear? Look at the flowers of the field. They do not spin thread or weave cloth. Yet not even King Solomon, in all his royal robes, was dressed as beautifully as one of these flowers.

"So do not worry about food or drink or clothes. God knows that you need all these things. If you will seek his kingdom and his righteousness, then all these things will be given to you as well.

"In all things, do unto others . . .

". . . as you would have them do unto you.

"You have heard people say, 'Love your neighbor and hate your enemy.'

"But I say, love your enemies, do good to those who hate you, and pray for those who hurt you so that you may be called children of God. Forgive those who sin against you, so that God will forgive you also.

"When you pray, do not pray just so that others will see you. Go into your room and close the door. Your heavenly Father, who sees all that is done in secret, will see you praying and will reward you.

"In your prayer, do not babble like the 'sinners,' who think they will be heard because of their many words. God knows what you need before you ask him. This, then, is how you should pray:

"Our Father, who art in heaven, hallowed be thy name.
Thy kingdom come. Thy will be done
on earth as it is in heaven.
Give us this day our daily bread.
And forgive us our debts, as we forgive our debtors.
And lead us not into temptation, but deliver us from evil.
For thine is the kingdom, and the power, and the glory forever.
Amen."

When Jesus finished saying all these things, the crowds were amazed.
Jesus got up and continued on his travels. And everywhere he went,
people gathered to hear his wonderful new message.